"Animals are such agreeable friends –
they ask no questions, they pass no criticisms."

George Elliot

The Animal
Songbook

Wise Publications
part of The Music Sales Group
London / New York / Paris / Sydney / Copenhagen / Madrid / Tokyo / Berlin

Published by
Wise Publications
8/9 Frith Street, London W1D 3JB, England.

Exclusive distributors:
Music Sales Limited
8/9 Frith Street, London, W1D 3JB, England.
Music Sales Corporation
257 Park Avenue South, New York, NY10010,
United States of America.
Music Sales Pty Limited
120 Rothschild Avenue, Rosebery, NSW 2018,
Australia.

Order No. AM983136
ISBN 1-84609-106-3
This book © Copyright 2005
Wise Publications, a division of Music Sales Limited.

Compiled & edited by Heather Ramage.
Music processed by Note-orious Productions Limited.
Designed & art directed by Michael Bell Design.
Illustrated by Sonia Canals.
Printed in China.

Your Guarantee of Quality:
As publishers, we strive to produce every
book to the highest commercial standards.
This book has been carefully designed to
minimise awkward page turns and to make playing
from it a real pleasure.
Throughout, the printing and binding have been
planned to ensure a sturdy, attractive publication
which should give years of enjoyment.
If your copy fails to meet our high standards,
please inform us and we will gladly replace it.

Acknowledgments:
The editor and publishers gratefully acknowledge
permission to reproduce the following copyright material:
'My Dog Spot' by Rodney Bennett.
Used with the kind permission of Mrs Anne E. Hay.

*Every effort has been made to trace the copyright holders
of the works in this book but one or two were unreachable.
We would be grateful if the rights owners concerned
would contact us.*

www.musicsales.com

Poems...

Stories...

Songs...

Alice The Camel

Traditional

1.Al-ice the ca-mel has five humps. Al-ice the ca-mel has
(Verses 2-6 see block lyric)

five humps. Al-ice the ca-mel has five humps so

go, Al-ice,— go. Boom, boom, boom, Al-ice is a horse!

2
Alice the camel has four humps.
Alice the camel has four humps.
Alice the camel has four humps
So go, Alice, go.
Boom, boom, boom.

3
Alice the camel has three humps.
Alice the camel has three humps.
Alice the camel has three humps
So go, Alice, go.
Boom, boom, boom.

4
Alice the camel has two humps.
Alice the camel has two humps.
Alice the camel has two humps
So go, Alice, go.
Boom, boom, boom.

5
Alice the camel has one hump.
Alice the camel has one hump.
Alice the camel has one hump
So go, Alice, go.
Boom, boom, boom.

6
Alice the camel has no humps.
Alice the camel has no humps.
Alice the camel has no humps
So Alice is a horse!

All The Pretty Little Horses

Traditional

Lullaby

Hush-you- bye, don't you cry, go to sleep-y, lit-tle ba - by.

When you wake, you shall have all the pret-ty lit-tle hors - es.

Blacks and bays, dap-ples and greys, coach and six-a-lit-tle hors - es.

Hush-you-bye, don't you cry, go to sleep-y, lit-tle ba - by.

All The Pretty Little Horses

Animal Fair

Traditional

Brightly, in two (𝅘𝅥𝅭 = one beat)

went to the an - i - mal fair, _____ the birds and the beasts were

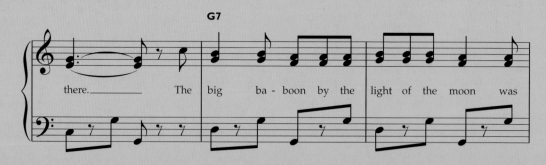

there._____ The big ba - boon by the light of the moon was

8

comb - ing his au - burn hair._____ The mon - key fell out of his

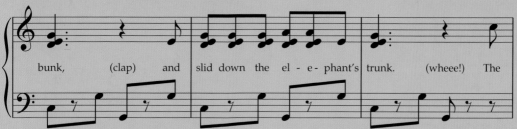

bunk, (clap) and slid down the el - e - phant's trunk. (wheee!) The

Em7   **Fmaj7**   **Em7**   **Fmaj7**   **G7**

el - e - phant sneezed and fell on his knees, and what be - came of the

C/G   **G7 C**   **G7**   **C**   **G7 C**   **G7**   **C N.C.**

mon - key, mon - key, mon - key, mon - key, monk?

G7

C

The monk?

Baa Baa Black Sheep

Traditional

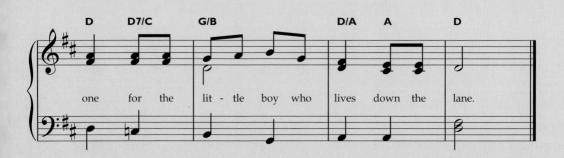

Chook Chook

Traditional

Moderately

1. Chook, chook, chook, chook, chook, "Good morn-ing Mrs__ Hen.
(Verses 2-5 see block lyric)

How ma-ny chick-ens have you got?" "Mad-am, I've got ten.

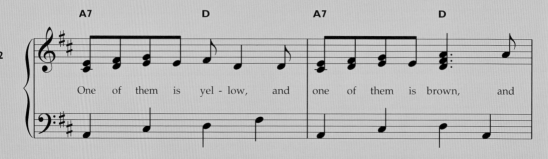

One of them is yel-low, and one of them is brown, and

The Animal Songbook

12

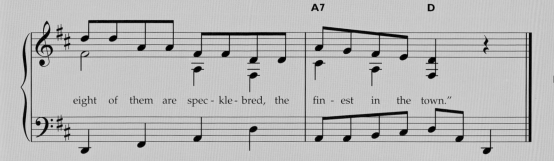

A7   **D**

eight of them are spec-kle-bred, the fin-est in the town."

2

Chook, chook, chook, chook, chook,
"Good morning Mrs Hen.
How many chickens have you got?"
"Madam, I've got ten.
Two of them are yellow,
And two of them are brown,
And six of them are speckle-bred,
The finest in the town."

3

Chook, chook, chook, chook, chook,
"Good morning Mrs Hen.
How many chickens have you got?"
"Madam, I've got ten.
Three of them are yellow,
And three of them are brown,
And four of them are speckle-bred,
The finest in the town."

4

Chook, chook, chook, chook, chook,
"Good morning Mrs Hen.
How many chickens have you got?"
"Madam, I've got ten.
Four of them are yellow,
And four of them are brown,
And two of them are speckle-bred,
The finest in the town."

5

Chook, chook, chook, chook, chook,
"Good morning Mrs Hen.
How many chickens have you got?"
"Madam, I've got ten.
Five of them are yellow,
And five of them are brown,
And none of them are speckle-bred,
The finest in the town."

Chook Chook

Bingo

Traditional

With a bounce

1. There was a farm-er, had a dog, and Bing-o was his name-o.

*B - I - N - G - O! B - I - N - G - O!

B - I - N - G - O! And Bing-o was his name - o.

Bingo

2
There was a farmer had a dog,
And Bingo was his name-o.
(Clap)-I-N-G-O!
(Clap)-I-N-G-O!
(Clap)-I-N-G-O!
And Bingo was his name-o!

3
There was a farmer had a dog,
And Bingo was his name-o.
(Clap, clap)-N-G-O!
(Clap, clap)-N-G-O!
(Clap, clap)-N-G-O!
And Bingo was his name-o!

4
There was a farmer had a dog,
And Bingo was his name-o.
(Clap, clap, clap)-G-O!
(Clap, clap, clap)-G-O!
(Clap, clap, clap)-G-O!
And Bingo was his name-o!

5
There was a farmer had a dog,
And Bingo was his name-o.
(Clap, clap, clap, clap)-O!
(Clap, clap, clap, clap)-O!
(Clap, clap, clap, clap)-O!
And Bingo was his name-o!

6
There was a farmer had a dog,
And Bingo was his name-o.
(Clap, clap, clap, clap, clap)
(Clap, clap, clap, clap, clap)
(Clap, clap, clap, clap, clap)
And Bingo was his name-o!

*As you sing through
verses 2-6, replace each letter
with a clap, as shown.*

Ding Dong Bell

Moderately   **Traditional**

Daddy Fox

Traditional

With movement

1.Dad-dy Fox went out on a chil - ly night, with a ling - tong dil - ly - dong
(Verses 2-7 see block lyric)

kye - ro - me; and he prayed for the moon to give him light, with a

ling - tong dil - ly - dong kye - ro - me. **f** Hey! Fa - la - le, fa - la-

Chorus

-la, fa - la - lay - ro. Hey! Fa - la - lay - ro, lay - ro - lee. Up jumps John,

Daddy Fox

Hey! Fa-la-le, fa-la-la,
Fa-la-lay-ro.
Hey! Fa-la-lay-ro, lay-ro-lee.
Chorus   *Up jumps John,*
Ringing on his bell,
With a ling-tong dilly-dong kye-ro-me.

2   Well, he ran till he came to a great big pen,
With a ling-tong dilly-dong kye-ro-me;
And the ducks and the geese were kept therein,
With a ling-tong dilly-dong kye-ro-me.

Chorus

3   He grabbed the grey goose by the neck,
With a ling-tong dilly-dong kye-ro-me;
And up with the little ones over his back,
With a ling-tong dilly-dong kye-ro-me.

Chorus

4   Old Mother Flipper-Flopper jumped out of bed,
With a ling-tong dilly-dong kye-ro-me;
Out of the window she stuck her little head,
With a ling-tong dilly-dong kye-ro-me.

Chorus

5   John, he ran to the top of the hill,
With a ling-tong dilly-dong kye-ro-me;
And he blew his little horn both loud and shrill,
With a ling-tong dilly-dong kye-ro-me.

Chorus

6   The fox, he ran to his cosy den,
With a ling-tong dilly-dong kye-ro-me;
And there were the little ones, eight, nine, ten,
With a ling-tong dilly-dong kye-ro-me.

Chorus

7   Then the fox and his wife, without any strife,
With a ling-tong dilly-dong kye-ro-me;
They cut up the goose with a carving knife,
With a ling-tong dilly-dong kye-ro-me.

Chorus

The Ugly Duckling

Hans Christian Andersen

Retold by Stuart Constable

There once was an ugly duckling. Actually, he was not really ugly, he was just different from his three brothers and his four sisters. But they called him ugly and even his mother, who should have known better, made him walk a long way behind when she took her ducklings down to the pond beside the farmyard.

It was not long before the poor little duckling began to feel very lonely and sad. He decided to leave his family and the other ducks on the pond and find somewhere else to live, where he would not be called names and teased just because he was not the same as everyone else.

The first place he found was a little cottage, where there lived a kind old woman.

"Why look at you, you funny little thing!" she said gently to him. "Here, why don't you come into the kitchen and have a drink of water and some bread?"

The little duckling followed the kind old woman into the warm kitchen and she placed a little saucer of water on the flag-stoned floor. Then she scattered some bread crumbs, which the duckling gobbled up hungrily, but he had only eaten a few morsels when he heard an angry hissing and clucking.

Into the kitchen stalked a proud cat and a fussing hen, who gazed haughtily at the frightened little duck.

"Call yourself a duckling!" snapped the hen. "I've never seen anything so ugly!" Meanwhile, the cat prowled around the duckling, his eyes alight with greed.

"Not too ugly to eat, mind…" he murmured.

At that moment, the little old woman came hurrying back into the kitchen.

"Go on, shoo!" she cried at the cat, but it was too late. The poor little duckling was already scuttling frantically out of the door.

He wandered on along the river bank, lonelier than ever, until he found a quiet marshy place where he lay down to sleep. When he awoke, he floated miserably out onto the river and stared at his reflection in the water.

"I am an ugly duckling," he said gloomily to himself.

Just then, his reflection disappeared with a rippling plop and a frog poked his head out of the water. "You certainly are," he chirruped, and went splashing away, croaking with laughter.

The poor duckling decided he would stay in his marshy place forever, away from anyone who would call him ugly or laugh at him. So he hid himself in the tall reeds of the bank, watching and waiting as the world passed him by and the seasons marked the turning of the year.

As the winter approached, he heard a great crying in the sky and he looked up to see a flock of snow-white swans making their majestic way along the river to their nesting places.

"If only I were as beautiful as those swans," sighed the duckling.

He looked down to see the frog staring scornfully at him again.

"Fat chance," croaked the frog, and plopped away before the duckling could reply.

Winter passed and still the duckling stayed hidden in his reeds. But when Spring began to roll her green carpet across the land, he found that it was not as easy to hide, because his head had risen above the tallest of the stems.

The duckling looked down once more and saw that the frog had come back to laugh at him again. But instead of sneering at the duckling, the frog was looking rather frightened.

"What's the matter," said the duckling, "have you no more insults to throw at me?"

"What, who me?" stammered the frog. "Me? Why no sir, not at all. Insults, sir? Why, not at all, the very idea, I wouldn't dream of such a thing, really I wouldn't, and I'm very sorry to have disturbed you sir, and if you'll excuse me I really must be going to talk to a toad about a fly…" And the frog crawled humbly away.

Puzzled, the ugly duckling stared after him, until suddenly he heard once again the haunting cry in the sky above. He looked up to see the swans soaring down and skimming gracefully to a halt on the river all around him. One of them swam demurely towards him.

"Why, good morning sir," she murmured. "We are honoured to have you among us."

"What, who me?" stammered the duckling.

"Indeed, yes," replied the swan, "for you are surely the most handsome of our kind we have encountered along the whole length of the river."

The duckling stared at her in confusion, and then a thought burst in his head like the breaking dawn. He coiled his long neck and gazed at his reflection in the water.

Gone were the stubby grey feathers and angry little beak. Instead, shimmering in the rippling river, he saw an elegant swan, whose white plumage glistened in the morning sunlight.

"Please," said the swan who had come to meet him. "Won't you fly with us?"

"I will," said the new swan, a duckling no more. And filled with joy, he spread his graceful wings and soared with her into the spring-blue sky.

22

The Tadpole

E. E. Gould

Underneath the water weeds
Small and black, I wriggle,
And life is most surprising!
Wiggle! Waggle! Wiggle!
There's every now and then a most
Exciting change in me,
I wonder, wiggle! Waggle!
What I shall turn out to be!

Eensy Weensy Spider

Traditional

Moderately

The een - sy ween - sy spi - der went

up the wat - er spout.

Down came the rain and

24

washed the spi - der out.

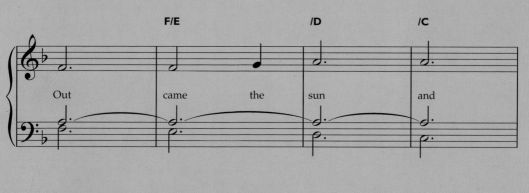

Out came the sun and

dried up all the rain. Now the

een - sy ween - sy spi - der went

up the spout a - gain.

Field Mice

Traditional

Swung feel

1. Down in the mea - dow where the long grass grows,___ there were
(Verses 2-5 see block lyric)

five lit - tle field mice wash - ing their clothes,_____ with a

rub - a - dub here and a rub - a - dub there,_ that's___ the way the field mice

Chorus

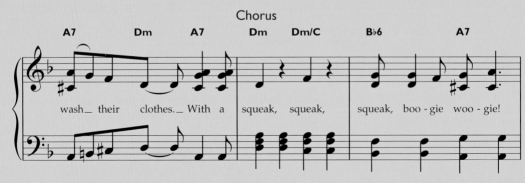

wash_ their clothes._ With a squeak, squeak, squeak, boo - gie woo - gie!

The Animal Songbook

Squeak, squeak, squeak, boo-gie woo-gie! Squeak, squeak,

squeak, boo-gie woo-gie! That's the way the field mice wash their clothes.

Field Mice

Chorus
With a squeak, squeak, squeak, boogie woogie!
Squeak, squeak, squeak, boogie woogie!
Squeak, squeak, squeak, boogie woogie!
That's the way the field mice wash their clothes.

2
Down in the meadow where the long grass grows,
There were four little field mice washing their clothes,
With a rub-a-dub here and a rub-a-dub there,
That's the way the field mice wash their clothes.

Chorus

3
Down in the meadow where the long grass grows,
There were three little field mice washing their clothes,
With a rub-a-dub here and a rub-a-dub there,
That's the way the field mice wash their clothes.

Chorus

4
Down in the meadow where the long grass grows,
There were two little field mice washing their clothes,
With a rub-a-dub here and a rub-a-dub there,
That's the way the field mice wash their clothes.

Chorus

5
Down in the meadow where the long grass grows,
There was one little field mouse washing his clothes,
With a rub-a-dub here and a rub-a-dub there,
That's the way the field mouse washes his clothes.

Chorus

Five Little Ducks

Traditional

Five Little Ducks

Moderately

1. Five lit - tle ducks went swim - ming one day,
(Verses 2-5 see block lyric)

ov - er the hills and far a - way. The mo - ther duck said, "Quack,

quack, quack, quack" and on - ly four lit - tle ducks came back.

2
Four little ducks went swimming one day,
Over the hills and far away.
The mother duck said, "Quack, quack, quack, quack"
And only three little ducks came back.

3
Three little ducks went swimming one day,
Over the hills and far away.
The mother duck said, "Quack, quack, quack, quack"
And only two little ducks came back.

4
Two little ducks went swimming one day,
Over the hills and far away.
The mother duck said, "Quack, quack, quack, quack"
And only one little duck came back.

5
One little duck went swimming one day,
Over the hills and far away.
The mother duck said, "Quack, quack, quack, quack"
And five little ducks came swimming right back.

Old MacDonald

Traditional

Bright

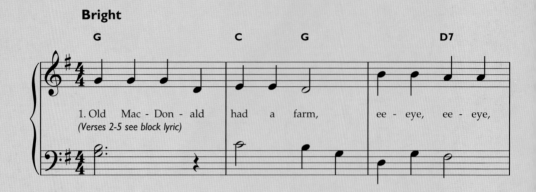

1. Old Mac-Don-ald had a farm, ee - eye, ee - eye,
(Verses 2-5 see block lyric)

oh! And on that farm he had some chicks,

Repeat as necessary

ee - eye, ee - eye, oh! With a chick - chick here, and a

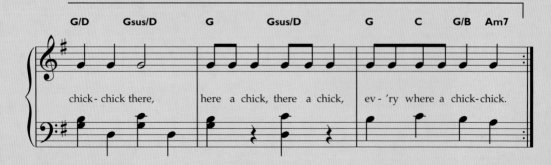

chick - chick there, here a chick, there a chick, ev - 'ry where a chick-chick.

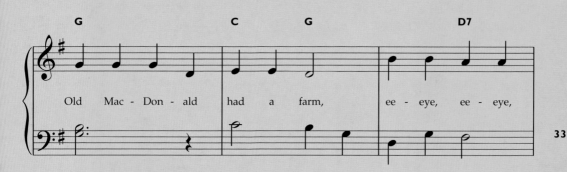

Old Mac - Don - ald   had   a   farm,   ee - eye, ee - eye,

|1-4
G
oh!

|5
G
oh!

2

Old MacDonald had a farm,
Ee-eye, ee-eye, oh!
And on that farm he had some ducks,
Ee-eye, ee-eye, oh!
With a quack-quack here and a quack-quack there,
Here a quack, there a quack, everywhere a quack-quack.
Chick-chick here and a chick-chick there,
Here a chick, there a chick, everywhere a chick-chick.
Old MacDonald had a farm,
Ee-eye, ee-eye, oh!

3

...and on that farm he had some cows...
With a moo-moo here and a moo-moo there,
Here a moo, there a moo, everywhere a moo-moo,
Quack-quack here and a quack-quack there...
Chick-chick here and a chick-chick there...

4

...and on that farm he had some pigs...
With an oink-oink here and an oink-oink there,
Here an oink, there an oink, everywhere an oink-oink,
Moo-moo here...
Quack-quack here...
Chick-chick here...

5

...and on that farm he had some sheep...
With a baa-baa here and a baa-baa there...
Oink-oink here...
Moo-moo here...
Quack-quack here...
Chick-chick here...

Have A Little Dog

Traditional

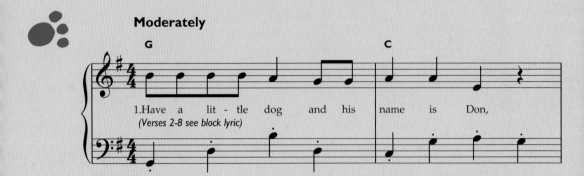

Moderately

1.Have a lit - tle dog and his name is Don,
(Verses 2-8 see block lyric)

(whistle) _____

Have a lit - tle dog and his name is Don. His legs go to feet and his bod - y goes to tongue. Toll - a -

winck - er, toll - a - winck - er, turn - toll - y - aye.

2 Have a little box about three feet square, *(whistle)*
Have a little box about three feet square,
When I go to travel I put him in there,
Toll-a-winker, toll-a-winker, tum-tolly-aye.

3 When I go to travel, I travel like an ox, *(whistle)*
When I go to travel, I travel like an ox,
And in that vest pocket I carry that box,
Toll-a-winker, toll-a-winker, tum-tolly-aye.

4 Had a little hen and her colour was fair, *(whistle)*
Had a little hen and her colour was fair,
Sat her on a bomb and she hatched me a hare,
Toll-a-winker, toll-a-winker, tum-tolly-aye.

5 The hare turned a horse about six feet high, *(whistle)*
The hare turned a horse about six feet high,
If you want to beat this you'll have to tell a lie,
Toll-a-winker, toll-a-winker, tum-tolly-aye.

6 I had a little mule and his name was Jack, *(whistle)*
I had a little mule and his name was Jack,
I rode him on his tail to save his back,
Toll-a-winker, toll-a-winker, tum-tolly-aye.

7 I had a little mule and his name was Jay, *(whistle)*
I had a little mule and his name was Jay,
I pulled his tail to hear him bray,
Toll-a-winker, toll-a-winker, tum-tolly-aye.

8 I had a little mule, he was made of hay, *(whistle)*
I had a little mule, he was made of hay,
First big wind come along and blew him away,
Toll-a-winker, toll-a-winker, tum-tolly-aye.

Have A Little Dog

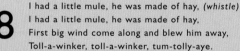

Five Little Speckled Frogs

Traditional

Moderately

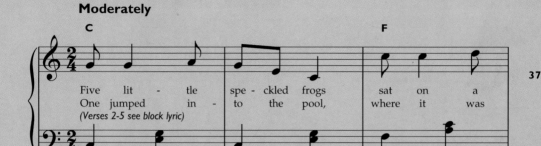

Five lit - tle spe - ckled frogs sat on a
One jumped in - to the pool, where it was

(Verses 2-5 see block lyric)

spe - ckled log, eat - ing some most de - li - cious
nice and cool, now there are

bugs. Yum! Yum! just four spe - ckled frogs. Glub! Glub!

2
Four little speckled frogs,
Sat on a speckled log,
Eating some most delicious bugs,
Yum! Yum!
One jumped into the pool,
Where it was nice and cool,
Now there are just three speckled frogs,
Glub! Glub!

3 Three little speckled frogs, *etc.*

4 Two little speckled frogs, *etc.*

5
One little speckled frog
Sat on a speckled log,
Eating some most delicious bugs,
Yum! Yum!
One jumped into the pool,
Where it was nice and cool,
Now there are no more speckled frogs,
Glub! Glub!

I Know An Old Lady
Who Swallowed A Fly

Traditional

1. I know an old la-dy who swal-lowed a fly, I don't know why she

swal-lowed a fly, per-haps she'll die! 2. I

know an old la-dy who swal-lowed a spi-der that wrig-gled and jig-gled and

(Verses 2-9 see block lyric)

Repeat as necessary

tickl-ed in-side her. She swal-lowed the spi-der to catch the fly, (she)

38

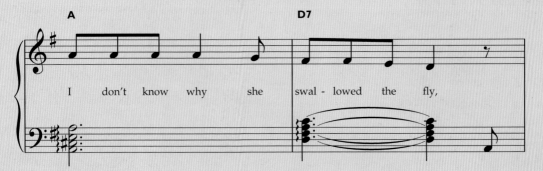

A   **D7**

I don't know why she swal - lowed the fly,

G   **Fine**   **D.S. al Fine**

per - haps she'll die!   2.I

2
I know an old lady who swallowed a spider
That wriggled and jiggled and tickled inside her.
She swallowed the spider to catch the fly,
I don't know why she swallowed a fly,
Perhaps she'll die!

3
I know an old lady who swallowed a bird.
How absurd, to swallow a bird!
She swallowed the bird to catch the spider
That wriggled, *etc.*

4
I know an old lady who swallowed a cat,
Just fancy that, she swallowed a cat!
She swallowed the cat to catch the bird,
She swallowed the bird to catch the spider, *etc.*

5
I know an old lady who swallowed a dog,
What a hog, to swallow a dog!
She swallowed the dog to catch the cat,
She swallowed the cat to catch the bird, *etc.*

6
I know an old lady who swallowed a goat.
She just opened her throat and swallowed a goat!
She swallowed the goat to catch the dog,
She swallowed the dog to catch the cat, *etc.*

7
I know an old lady who swallowed a cow.
I don't know HOW she swallowed a cow.
She swallowed the cow to catch the goat,
She swallowed the goat to catch the dog, *etc.*

8
I know an old lady who swallowed a rhinoceros,
THAT'S PREPOSTEROUS!!
She swallowed the rhino to catch the cow,
She swallowed the cow to catch the goat, *etc.*

9
I know an old lady who swallowed a horse.
She's dead, of course.

Puss In Boots

Charles Perrault

Retold by Ruth Playford

Once upon a time, there was a miller who had three sons. When he died, he left his mill to his oldest son, his donkey to his second son and his cat to his youngest son.

"Oh dear, Puss," said the youngest son to the cat, "how are we going to feed ourselves with no money?"

"Leave it to me, master," said Puss, and taking a pair of boots and a bag he went to the nearest lettuce field and picked the juiciest lettuce he could find. He put the lettuce inside the bag and lay in wait. Soon a plump rabbit came to eat the lettuce. Puss swiftly caught the rabbit and took it to the King's palace.

"Here is a fine rabbit as a present for you from my master, the Marquis of Carrabas," said Puss to the King. The King was very pleased with the present.

The next day the King and his daughter were driving by the river. Puss hurried to his master and told him to take off his clothes and swim in the river.

"You must pretend that you are the Marquis of Carrabas," said Puss. The miller's son scratched his head and agreed to the plan.

As the King's carriage drew near, Puss hailed the King and said, "My master, the Marquis of Carrabas is swimming in the river and thieves have run off with his clothes." The King stopped the carriage and told his servants to hurry to the castle and fetch some clothes for the Marquis of Carrabas.

When the clothes arrived, the Marquis put them on and rode in the carriage with the King and his daughter. Puss hurried along the road and came to a field with men working in it. He stopped and said, "The King is driving in his carriage along this road, when he stops and asks you who this land belongs to, tell him it belongs to the Marquis of Carrabas."

As the King approached the field he stopped the carriage and asked the men who the land belonged to.

"The Marquis of Carrabas, your majesty," said the men. The King was very impressed.

Puss had found out that the land belonged to a terrible ogre who lived in a castle further along. He hurried to the door and knocked. When the ogre answered, he said,

"I hear you are a great magician, sir."

"I am," roared the ogre and turned himself into a snarling lion. Puss jumped in fright.

"It must be easy to turn yourself into something so big," he said. "Can you turn yourself into something small, like a mouse?"

"Of course I can," roared the ogre and quickly turned into a mouse. Puss pounced and gobbled the mouse up. That was the end of the ogre!

As the King's carriage reached the castle, Puss threw open the doors and said,

"Welcome to the Marquis of Carrabas's house." The King was very impressed and thought what a fine husband the Marquis would make for his daughter.

So they were married and lived happily every after!

Puss In Boots

Goosey, Goosey, Gander

Traditional

Goos-ey, goos-ey, gan - der, whi-ther shall I wan - der?

Up - stairs and down - stairs and in my la-dy's cham - ber.

There I met an old man who would not say his prayers. So I

took him by the left leg and threw him down the stairs.

Hark, Hark, The Dogs Do Bark

Traditional

Little Bird

Traditional

Steadily

1. Lit - tle bird, *(Verse 2 see block lyric)* lit - tle bird, go through my win - dow,

lit - tle bird, lit - tle bird, go through my win - dow,

46

lit - tle bird, lit - tle bird, go through my win - dow and

buy mo - lass - es can - dy. Go

Em7   F#m   Em   A

through   my   win - dow,   my   su - gar   lump,   go

Em7   F#m   D

through   my   win - dow,   my   su - gar   lump,   and

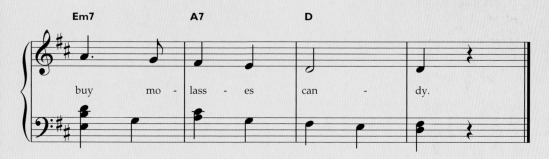

Em7   A7   D

buy   mo - lass - es   can - dy.

2

Blue bird, blue bird,
Fly through my window,
Blue bird, blue bird,
Fly through my window,
Blue bird, blue bird,
Fly through my window,
And buy molasses candy.

Chorus
Fly through my window,
My little bird,
Fly through my window,
My little bird,
And buy molasses candy.

Ladybird, Ladybird

Traditional

Steadily

Ladybird, ladybird, fly away home, your house is on fire and your children are gone.

Bunny creeps out and caresses his nose,
Combs out his ears with his fluttering toes,
Blinks at the sun
And commences to run
With a skip and a hop
And a flippety-flop,
Nibbling the clover wherever he goes;
But only when he is quite easy in mind
Does he button his little white tail down behind.

Bunny Rabbit
Anonymous

Bunny stops dead and stiffens each hair,
And his eyelids freeze in a terrified stare,
And he pricks up his ears,
For the sound that he hears
Is a low muffled beat
And a drumming of feet
And an ominous rub-a-dub-dubbing – but where?
He's off like the wind! He's off like the wind!
And his little white tail is unbuttoned behind.

Old Blue

Traditional

Moderately

1.Had an old dog and his name was Blue.
(Verses 2-9 see block lyric)

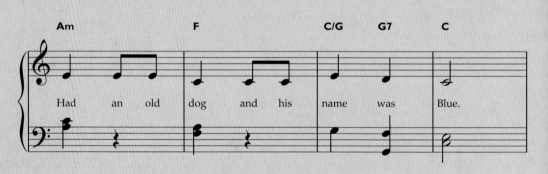

Had an old dog and his name was Blue.

Had an old dog and his name was Blue.

50

Bet you five dol-lars was a good dog, too.

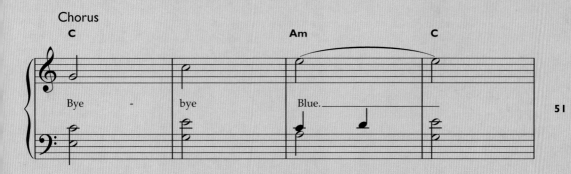

Chorus   *Bye bye Blue.*
You're a good dog, you.

2 Every night just about dark *(3 times)*
Blue goes out and begins to bark.

Chorus

3 Everything just in a rush *(3 times)*
He treed a possum in a white-oak bush.

Chorus

4 Possum walked out to the end of a limb *(3 times)*
Blue set down and talked to him.

Chorus

5 Blue got sick and very sick *(3 times)*
Sent for the doctor to come here quick.

Chorus

6 Doctor come and he come in a run *(3 times)*
Says, "Old Blue, your hunting's done."

Chorus

7 Blue he died and died so hard *(3 times)*
Scratched little holes all around the yard.

Chorus

8 Laid him out in a shady place *(3 times)*
Covered him o'er with a possum's face.

Chorus

9 When I get to heaven I'll tell you what I'll do *(3 times)*
I'll take my horn and blow for Blue.

Chorus

Oh Where Has My Little Dog Gone?

Words by Septimus Winner
Music: Traditional

Moderately

Oh where, oh where has my lit - tle dog gone? Oh

where, oh where can he be?_____ With his

ears cut short and his tail cut long, oh

where, oh where can he be?_____

Ride A Cock Horse

Traditional

Moderately

Ride a cock - horse to Ban - bu - ry cross, to

see a fine la - dy ride on a white horse.

Rings on her fin - gers and bells on her toes and

she shall have mu - sic wher - ev - er she goes.

Old Hogan's Goat

Traditional

Moderately

1. There was a man, (there was a *(Verses 2-3 see block lyric)* man), now please take

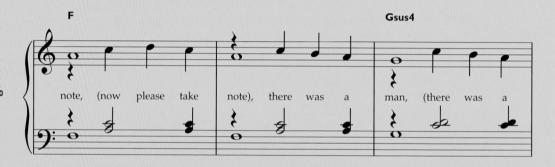

note, (now please take note), there was a man, (there was a

man), who had a goat, (who had a goat). He loved that

goat, (he loved that goat), in - deed he did, (in - deed he

The Animal Songbook

Gsus4   G7

did), he loved that | goat, (he loved that | goat), just like a

C   G7   1-2   C   N.C.   3

kid, (just like a | kid). 2.One day that | train).

Second voice in brackets

2

One day that goat... *(one day that goat)*
Was feeling fine... *(was feeling fine)*
Ate three red shirts... *(ate three red shirts)*
From off the line... *(from off the line)*
The old man grabbed... *(the old man grabbed)*
Her by the back... *(her by the back)*
And tied her to... *(and tied her to)*
The railway track... *(the railway track)*

3

Now when the train... *(now when the train)*
Came into sight... *(came into sight)*
The goat grew pale... *(the goat grew pale)*
And grey with fright... *(and grey with fright)*
She struggled hard... *(she struggled hard)*
And then again... *(and then again)*
Coughed up the shirts... *(coughed up the shirts)*
And flagged the train... *(and flagged the train)*

The Ostrich And The Hedgehog

Traditional African Tale
Retold by Ruth Playford

One lovely day, a hedgehog decided to go and visit a field of barley and see how tall it had grown. He had seen it grow from very small, green shoots and was sure it was now very tall and ready to be harvested. When he got to the barley he gave a great big sigh, for it was taller than he had imagined – a wonderful golden sight!

As he stood there, he saw a big bird coming towards him, it was an ostrich. Ostriches cannot fly but they can run very fast. The hedgehog smiled and said, "Good morning."

The ostrich looked down and grumpily said, "I don't talk to short-legged creatures like you."

"I may be short-legged," said the hedgehog, "but I can run faster than any other animal around here."

"No-one can run as fast me," said the ostrich.

The hedgehog smiled.

"Really?" he said, "why don't we have a race and see who is the fastest?"

"Fine," said the ostrich, "Let's go now, on your marks, get set…"

"No," said the hedgehog, "I haven't had my breakfast yet, I can't run on an empty stomach. Let's meet back here at midday and race up and down the rows of barley."

The ostrich smiled and nodded, thinking how easy it was going to be racing such a short-legged creature. He put his head in the sand and had a nap.

The hedgehog raced home and called all of his family to join him; his brothers, his sisters, his aunts, his uncles, his mother and his father.

"You must help me beat the ostrich in a race," he said.

"Run faster than an ostrich?" asked his cousin, "that's impossible."

"Not if you follow my plan," said the hedgehog.

"Each of you must stand at the end of a row of barley. I will start the race with the ostrich but only run a short way and then turn back, as the ostrich comes near, pretend to run and be out of breath. He will think it's me beating him every time."

At midday the hedgehogs went to stand in their positions. The ostrich woke up and joined the hedgehog at the start. "Are you ready?" he asked. The hedgehog nodded.

"On your marks, get set, go…" shouted the ostrich and sprinted off, leaving the hedgehog far behind. But as he came near the the end of the row, he saw the hedgehog, puffing and panting in front of him. The ostrich ran down the next row and again the hedgehog was in front of him. The ostrich ran faster and faster, but the hedgehog was always ahead. He didn't realise that several hedgehogs and not just one were beating him! As he ran along the last row of barley, he saw in front of him the hedgehog looking rather bored and saying, "Here you are at last." The ostrich was very embarrassed and confused and walked off, very tired and with two sore feet from running the fastest he had ever run. No one saw him for a long time after that!

Two Little Dickie Birds

Traditional

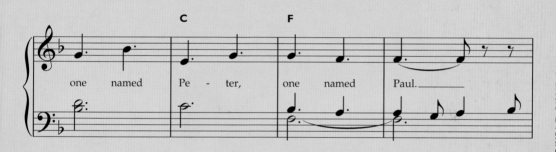

The Ants Came Marching

Traditional

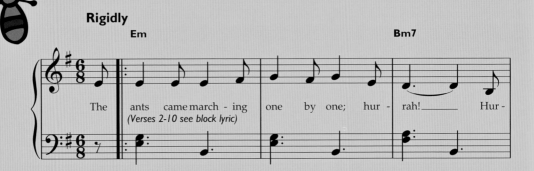

The ants came march - ing one by one; hur - rah!____ Hur -

(Verses 2-10 see block lyric)

- rah!____ The ants came march - ing one by one; hur - rah!____ Hu -

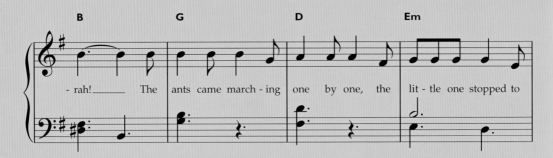

- rah!____ The ants came march - ing one by one, the lit - tle one stopped to

62

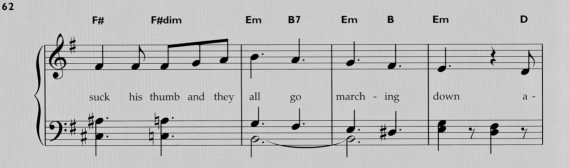

suck his thumb and they all go march - ing down a -

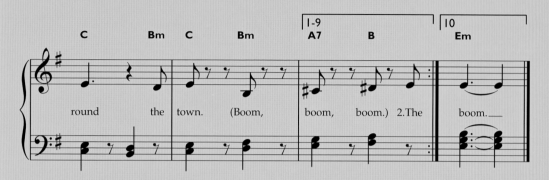

round   the town.   (Boom,   boom,   boom.) 2.The   boom.___

2

The ants came marching two by two; Hurrah! Hurrah!
The ants came marching two by two; Hurrah! Hurrah!
The ants came marching two by two,
The little one stopped to tie his shoe,
And they all go marching down around the town.
Boom, boom, boom.

3

The ants came marching three by three; Hurrah! Hurrah!
The ants came marching three by three; Hurrah! Hurrah!
The ants came marching three by three,
The little one stopped to climb a tree,
And they all go marching down around the town.
Boom, boom, boom.

4

The ants came marching four by four...
The little one stopped to shut the door...

5

The ants came marching five by five...
The little one stopped to take a dive...

6

The ants came marching six by six...
The little one stopped to pick up sticks...

7

The ants came marching seven by seven...
The little one stopped to go to heaven...

8

The ants came marching eight by eight...
The little one stopped to shut the gate...

9

The ants came marching nine by nine...
The little one stopped to scratch his spine...

10

The ants came marching ten by ten...
The little one stopped to say "the end"...

The Ants Came Marching

One Elephant

Traditional

Moderately

One* el - e - phant went out to play up - on a spi - der's

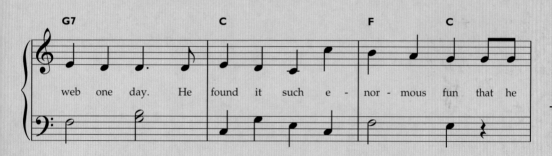

web one day. He found it such e - nor - mous fun that he

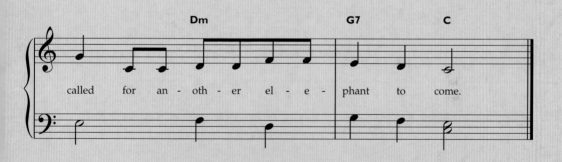

called for an - oth - er el - e - phant to come.

Amend number accordingly

Instructions

Get everyone into a circle. Pick one person to be the elephant and ask them to stand in the middle.

While singing, the elephant in the middle skips around having fun.

Those on the outside can mime appropriate actions to match the song.

On the line, "that he called for another elephant to come", everyone wiggles their bottom and the elephant in

the middle points at someone to come and join him/her. Keep going until everyone is an elephant!

Mary Had A Little Lamb

Traditional

Moderately

1. Mar - y had a lit - tle lamb, lit - tle lamb,
(Verses 3-8 see block lyric)

lit - tle lamb, Mar - y had a lit - tle lamb, its

fleece as white as snow. 2. And ev - 'ry - where that

Mar - y went, Mar - y went, Mar - y went, ev - 'ry - where that

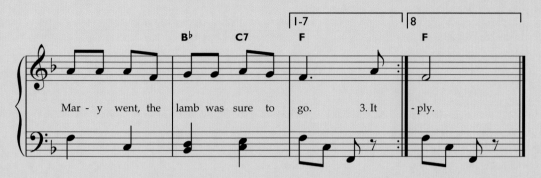

Mar - y went, the | lamb was sure to | go.   3. It | - ply.

3 It followed her to school one day,
School one day, school one day.
It followed her to school one day,
Which was against the rules.

4 It made the children laugh and play,
Laugh and play, laugh and play.
It made the children laugh and play,
To see a lamb at school.

5 And so the teacher turned it out,
Turned it out, turned it out.
And so the teacher turned it out,
But still it lingered near.

6 And waited patiently about,
'Ly about, 'ly about.
And waited patiently about,
Till Mary did appear.

7 Why does the lamb love Mary so?
Mary so, Mary so?
Why does the lamb love Mary so?
The eager children cry.

8 Why, Mary loves the lamb, you know,
Lamb, you know, lamb, you know.
Why, Mary loves the lamb, you know,
The teacher did reply.

The Barnyard Song

Traditional

Lively

1. I had a cat, and the cat pleased me, I

fed my cat un-der yon-der tree;

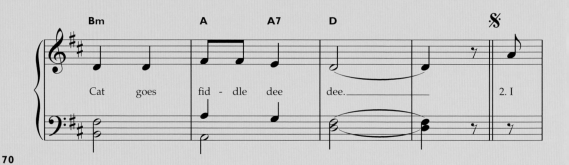

Cat goes fid-dle dee dee. 2. I

70

D   A7/E   D/F#   A7/E

had a hen, and the hen pleased me, I
(Verses 3-6 see block lyric)

fed   my   hen   un - der   yon - der   tree;

Repeat as necessary

Bm   F#m   G   Bm

Hen   goes   chim - my chuck,   chim - my chuck;   Cat   goes

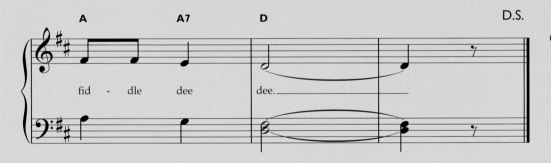

A   A7   D   D.S.

fid - dle   dee   dee.

3 I had a duck, *etc.*
...Duck goes quack, quack, quack, quack,
Hen goes chimmy chuck, chimmy chuck,
Cat goes fiddle dee dee.

4 I had a pig, *etc.*
...Pig goes oink, oink, oink, oink,
Duck goes quack, quack, quack, quack,
Hen goes chimmy chuck, chimmy chuck,
Cat goes fiddle dee dee.

5 I had a sheep, *etc.*
...Sheep goes baaa, baaa, baaa, baaa,
Pig goes oink, oink, oink, oink,
Duck goes quack, quack, quack, quack,
Hen goes chimmy chuck, chimmy chuck,
Cat goes fiddle dee dee.

6 I had a turkey, *etc.*
...Turkey goes gibble-gobble, gibble-gobble,
Sheep goes baaa, baaa, baaa, baaa,
Pig goes oink, oink, oink, oink,
Duck goes quack, quack, quack, quack,
Hen goes chimmy chuck, chimmy chuck,
Cat goes fiddle dee dee.

One, Two, Three, Four, Five

Traditional

Moderately

1. One, two, three, four, five, once I caught a fish a - live.
(Verse 2 see block lyric)

Six, seven, eight, nine, ten, then I let it go a - gain.

2
Why did you let it go?
Because it bit my finger so.
Which finger did it bite?
This little finger on the right.

The Curliest Thing
Anonymous

The squirrel is the curliest thing
I think I ever saw;
He curls his back, he curls his tail,
He curls each little paw,
He curls his little vest so white,
His little coat so grey –
He is the most curled-up wee soul
Out in the woods at play!

The Bear Went Over The Mountain

Traditional

Moderately

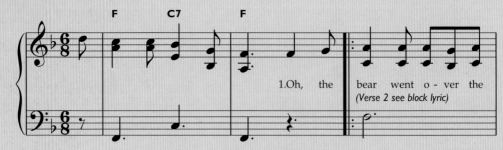

1.Oh, the bear went o - ver the
(Verse 2 see block lyric)

moun - tain, the bear went o - ver the moun - tain, the

74

bear went o - ver the moun - tain to see what he could

see.   To   see   what   he   could   see,_____   to

see   what   he   could   see.   Oh,   the   bear   went o - ver the

moun - tain   to   see what   he could   see.   2.Oh, he   see.

The Bear Went Over The Mountain

2

Oh, he saw another mountain,
He saw another mountain,
He saw another mountain and that's what he could see.
And that's what he could see,
And that's what he could see,
Oh, he saw another mountain and that's what he could see.

The Town Mouse And The Country Mouse

Aesop
Retold by Ruth Playford

76

Country Mouse lived in a nice quiet house in the roots of a tree. One day, his cousin Town Mouse came to stay.

"You will like it here," said Country Mouse, "it is nice and quiet."

He made a big supper for Town Mouse, but Town Mouse found the food too plain and simple. When Town Mouse went to bed, he found the bed was made of straw and it made him scratch and sneeze. It was very dark and too quiet; he couldn't get to sleep.

Early the next morning, Country Mouse was up gathering food for the winter. Town Mouse didn't like gathering food and getting his clothes and hands dirty.

"There's no need to look for food in the town," he said.

The next day they went to gather mushrooms and a horse tried to make friends with them. Town Mouse was so scared that he slipped over in a puddle. On the way home, Town Mouse talked about the town and how it was much better than the countryside. He was so busy talking that he didn't notice an owl swooping down towards them.

"Watch out," cried Country Mouse and pushed his cousin into the ditch. It was very close but they were safe.

Town Mouse hated the countryside even more after that and thought it was cold, wet and dangerous. He persuaded Country Mouse to visit the town and they hitched a lift with a car and hid until they arrived in the town.

The bright lights and the noise were very strange to Country Mouse. Town Mouse's house was very big and they prepared a big feast with cakes, puddings, cream and lots of other rich and sweet foods. Country Mouse felt sick from so much food and wished he could have the plain food he was used to. The next day Country Mouse found some cheese and went to eat it. Just in time, Town Mouse pushed him away and saved him from being caught in a mousetrap. As they ran away, a cat came around the corner and pounced. They managed to escape, but Country Mouse was very scared.

That night Country Mouse tried to sleep, but he didn't like the soft bed and the streetlights that shone into his room; he was homesick for his tree and the countryside.

The next day, the mice found a hamper underneath the Christmas tree.

"It's addressed to someone who lives near you," said Town Mouse.

Country Mouse jumped inside and waited until it was put inside a van and driven to near his home. When he got out and saw his village and the trees and heard the carols in the church, he sighed with happiness and thought how nice it was to be back home, and although he had enjoyed his adventures, he wouldn't be leaving the countryside for a very long time!

Ten Little Pigs

Traditional

1. Ten lit - tle pigs went to mar - ket,
(Verses 2-5 see block lyric)

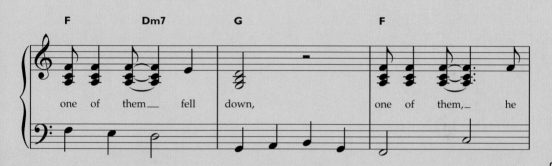

one of them___ fell down, one of them,___ he

ran a - way,___ how man - y got to town? Eight!___

2
Eight little pigs went to market,
One of them fell down,
One of them, he ran away,
How many got to town?
Six!

3
Six little pigs went to market,
One of them fell down,
One of them, he ran away,
How many got to town?
Four!

4
Four little pigs went to market,
One of them fell down,
One of them, he ran away,
How many got to town?
Two!

5
Two little pigs went to market,
One of them fell down,
One of them, he ran away,
How many got to town?
None!

Pussy Cat

Traditional

The Owl And The Pussy-Cat

Traditional

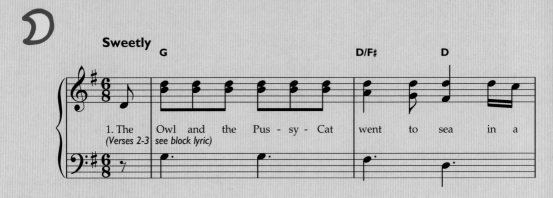

Sweetly

1. The Owl and the Pus-sy-Cat went to sea in a
(Verses 2-3 *see block lyric*)

beau-ti-ful pea-green boat; they took some hon-ey and

plen-ty of mon-ey wrapped up in a five pound note. The

Owl looked up to the stars a-bove, and sang to a small gui-

82

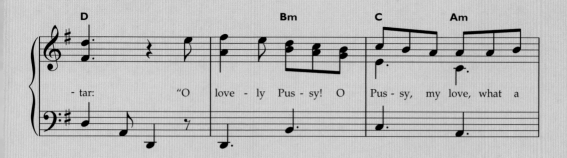

-tar: "O love-ly Pus-sy! O Pus-sy, my love, what a

beau-ti-ful Pus-sy you are,_____ you are,_____ you

a tempo

are._____ What a beau-ti-ful Pus-sy you are."_____

Pussy said to the Owl: "You elegant fowl,
How charmingly sweet you sing!
Oh, let us be married; too long we have tarried;
But what shall we do for a ring?"
They sailed away for a year and a day
To the land where the bong tree grows;
And there in the woods, a piggy-wig stood
With a ring at the end of his nose,
His nose,
His nose,
With a ring at the end of his nose.

2

"Dear Pig, are you willing to sell for one shilling
Your ring?" Said the piggy, "I will."
So they took it away, and were married next day
By the turkey who lives on the hill.
They dined on mince and slices of quince,
Which they ate with a runcible spoon,
And hand in hand on the edge of the sand,
They danced by the light of the moon,
The moon,
The moon,
They danced by the light of the moon.

3

Two Little Chickens

Traditional

Moderately

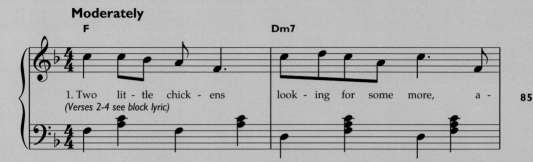

1. Two lit-tle chick-ens look-ing for some more, a-
(Verses 2-4 see block lyric)

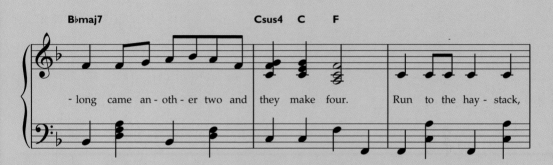

-long came an-oth-er two and they make four. Run to the hay-stack,

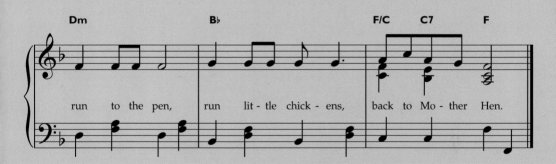

run to the pen, run lit-tle chick-ens, back to Mo-ther Hen.

2 Four little chickens getting in a fix,
Along came another two and they make six.
Run to the haystack, run to the pen,
Run little chickens, back to Mother Hen.

3 Six little chickens perching on a gate,
Along came another two and they make eight.
Run to the haystack, run to the pen,
Run little chickens, back to Mother Hen.

4 Eight little chickens run to Mother Hen,
Along came another two and they make ten.
Run to the haystack, run to the pen,
Run little chickens, back to Mother Hen.

Pop Goes The Weasel

Traditional

Half   a   pound   of   two - pen - ny   rice,

half   a   pound   of   trea - cle,   that's   the   way   the

mon - ey   goes,   pop   goes   the   wea - sel.

The Caterpillar
Christina Rossetti

Brown and furry
Caterpillar in a hurry,
Take your walk
To the shady leaf, or stalk,
Or what not,
Which may be the chosen spot.
No toad to spy you,
Hovering bird of prey pass by you;
Spin and die,
To live again a butterfly.

Three Little Kittens

Traditional

Moderately

1.Once three lit - tle kit - tens they lost their mit - tens, and
(Verses 2-4 see block lyric)

they be - gan to cry:_____ "Oh, moth - er dear, we

sad - ly fear our mit - tens we have lost!"_____ "What!

88

Lost your mit - tens! You naugh - ty kit - tens! Then

Cm/G   D/F#   G7/F   C7/E   F7

you   shall   have   no   pie." ___   "Meow! ___

89

Bb   F7   Bb

Meow! ___   Meow! ___   Meow!" ___

2 The three little kittens, they found their mittens,
And they began to cry:
"Oh, mother dear, see here, see here!
Our mittens we have found!"
"What? Found your mittens? You darling kittens!
Then you shall have some pie!"
"Meow, meow, meow, meow!"

3 The three little kittens put on their mittens,
And soon ate up their pie,
"Oh, mother dear, we greatly fear,
Our mittens we have soiled!"
"What? Soiled your mittens? You naughty kittens!"
Then they began to sigh,
"Meow, meow, meow, meow!"

4 The three little kittens, they washed their mittens,
And hung them up to dry.
"Oh, mother dear, look here, look here!
Our mittens we have washed!"
"What? Washed your mittens? You darling kittens!
But I smell a rat close by.
Hush, hush, hush, hush."

Three Little Kittens

This Little Pig Went To Market

Traditional

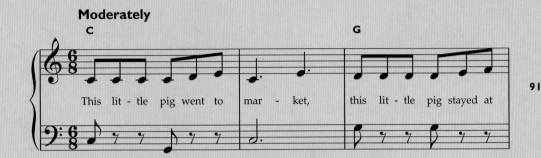

This lit - tle pig went to mar - ket, this lit - tle pig stayed at

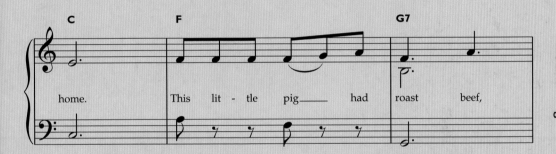

home. This lit - tle pig____ had roast beef,

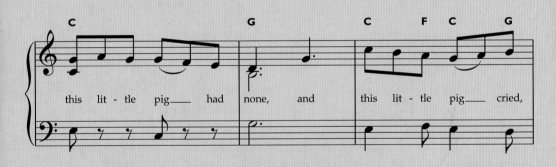

this lit - tle pig____ had none, and this lit - tle pig____ cried,

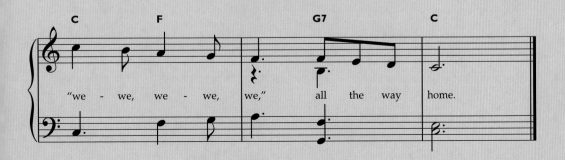

"we - we, we - we, we," all the way home.

Why Doesn't My Goose?

Traditional

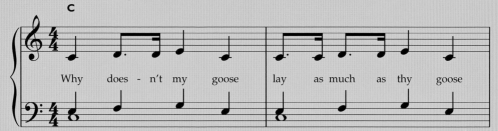

Why does - n't my goose lay as much as thy goose

when I paid for my goose twice as much as thine?

I have a white dog
Whose name is Spot,
And he's sometimes white
And he's sometimes not.
But whether he's white
Or whether he's not,
There's a patch on his ear
That makes him Spot.

My Dog, Spot
Rodney Bennett

He has a tongue
That is long and pink,
And he lolls it out
When he wants to think,
He seems to think most
When the weather is hot.
He's a wise sort of dog,
Is my dog, Spot.

He likes a bone
And he likes a ball,
But he doesn't care
For a cat at all.
He waggles his tail
And he knows what's what,
So I'm glad that he's my dog,
My dog, Spot.

The Three Billy Goats Gruff

Traditional

Retold by Stuart Constable

Once upon a time there was a great, green meadow which stood beside a mighty rushing river. In the meadow lived the three Billy Goats Gruff.

The first Billy Goat Gruff was small and quick. He had bright, beady eyes that were always looking for something new to see. His brown fluffy coat was speckled with white and his little horns were shiny and new.

The second Billy Goat Gruff was bigger and her eyes twinkled with kindness. She had a warm, glossy coat of white and two sharp horns.

The third Billy Goat Gruff was the biggest of all. He had a stern face and a heavy brown coat and his curving horns were gnarled and strong.

Every day, the Billy Goats Gruff would graze happily in the great, green meadow, cropping the juicy grass. Then, one day, the first Billy Goat Gruff wandered to the banks of the mighty rushing river and gazed across it with his keen, beady eyes.

On the other side, the grass looked still greener and juicier, and it was dotted with buttercups that were bright as the sun. So, the first Billy Goat Gruff trotted along the bank to the old wooden bridge and set off across the mighty rushing river.

But when he got to the middle of the bridge, a booming voice echoed from below.

"Oi!" it said. "Oi! Where do you think you're going, rattling your hooves on my bridge and waking me up?"

And out from under the bridge came the most disgusting troll you have ever seen. His eyes were blood-red, his lips were flabby and purple and his nose was a slimey green. His rust-coloured skin was lumpy and hairy and he smelled as if he had not had a bath for a very long time, even though he lived by the river.

The little goat was very scared. "Oh dear," he thought. "Oh dear, oh dear, oh dear."

The troll glared down at the first Billy Goat Gruff and licked his lips.

"Ah!" he said. "You appear to be my breakfast!"

The first Billy Goat Gruff thought as quickly as his darting, beady eyes.

"What, me?" he said. "Me? Why eat me when my friend, who is much bigger and tastier than me, is just coming?"

"Where?" said the troll, with a foul green liquid dribbling down his chin. Before the troll could catch him, the little goat galloped across the bridge with a clatter of rattling hooves. The troll roared with anger, but he could not catch the quick little goat.

The second Billy Goat Gruff heard the roaring of the troll and hurried to the bridge. When she saw the first Billy Goat Gruff on the other side she galloped across to help him. But when she got to the middle of the bridge, once again the booming voice echoed from below.

"Oi!" it said. "Oi! Where do you think you're going, rattling your hooves on my bridge and waking me up?" And once again the disgusting troll towered over the bridge, terrifying the poor Billy Goat Gruff at his feet.

"Ah!" said the troll. "You appear to be my lunch!"

The second Billy Goat Gruff thought as sharply as her elegant little horns.

"What, me?" she said. "Me? Why eat me when my friend, who is much bigger and tastier than me, is just coming?"

"Where?" said the troll, with clouds of stinking smoke puffing from his ears. Before the troll could catch her, the clever goat galloped across the bridge with a clatter of rattling hooves. The troll roared with anger, but he could not catch the bright white goat.

The third Billy Goat Gruff heard the roaring of the troll and hurried to the bridge. When he saw his two friends on the other side, he galloped across to join them.

But when he got to the middle of the bridge, the same booming voice echoed from below.

"Oi!" it said. "Oi! Where do you think you're going, rattling your hooves on my bridge and waking me up?" Once more the hideous troll towered over the bridge.

"Ah!" said the troll. "You appear to be my dinner!"

The third Billy Goat Gruff, however, was not scared at all. "Oh yeah?" he snarled and lowered his mighty head, pointing his gnarled and curving horns at the troll.

"Oh dear," thought the troll. "Oh dear, oh dear, oh d…" But he could not finish the last thought, because the third Billy Goat's horns caught him firmly in the tummy and sent him crashing into the mighty rushing river. He was carried away roaring with anger, but smelling better than he had for years.

With a satisfied toss of his head, the great big Billy Goat Gruff trotted across the bridge to join his friends in the greener, juicier grass on the other side. And the cruel and greedy troll was never seen (or smelled) again.

Kindness To Animals
Anonymous

Little children, never give
Pain to things that feel and live:
Let the gentle robin come
For the crumbs you save at home –
As his meat you throw along
He'll repay you with a song;
Never hurt the timid hare
Peeping from her green grass lair,
Let her come and sport and play
On the lawn at close of day;
The little lark goes soaring high
To the bright windows of the sky,
Singing as if 'twere always Spring,
And fluttering on an untired wing –
Oh! Let him sing his happy song,
Nor do these gentle creatures wrong.